HOW THEY LIVED

A SAMURAI WARRIOR

ANNE STEEL

Illustrated by
John James

ROURKE ENTERPRISES INC.
Vero Beach, Florida 32964

Printed in Belgium.

Library of Congress Cataloging-in-Publication Data

Steel, Anne.
    A Samurai warrior / Anne Steel ; illustrated by John James.
        p.   cm. -- (How they lived)
    Bibliography: p.
    Includes index.
    Summary: Describes the lives of Samurai warriors in seventeenth
century Japan.
    ISBN 0–86592–145–8
    1. Samurai--Juvenile literature.   [1. Samurai.   2. Japan--Social
life and customs--1600–1868.]   I. James, John, 1959- ill.
II. Title.   III. Series: How they lived (Vero Beach, Fla.)
DS827.S3S73 1988   87–38308
305.5′2—dc19   CIP
                                                     AC

CONTENTS

A CRUEL WARRIOR

The battle raged fiercely under the burning Japanese sun, as a strange and terrible figure pulled his panting horse to a halt. He wore brightly decorated armor, and his face was hidden by a frightening mask. Another mounted warrior appeared in the distance. The two men galloped straight toward each other and met with a sickening crash that knocked both of them to the ground. Quickly they untied their leg armor and drew their long swords. Their blades flashed back and forth with lightening speed. The air was filled with their harsh cries and the clash of metal. Then one fell slowly to the ground. With a single sweep of his sword, the victor cut off the dead man's head and held it up in triumph.

The year was A.D. 1610. The warriors were Samurai. Japan was torn by struggles between the armies of rival warlords. The Samurai were the most respected of these armies. They were mounted warriors, famous for their skill and courage in battle, their loyalty to their lord and their complete devotion to a code of conduct that preferred death to dishonor. Yet, there was another side to the Samurai's life. In more peaceful times, warriors would write poetry, make wonderful gardens or spend hours gazing at the beauty of the moon or a cherry blossom. For many centuries, these frightening, fascinating men were the most powerful people in Japan.

Samurai warriors grouped together into rival clans, which often fought wars against each other.

A Samurai's helmet and face-mask were designed to terrify the enemy.

THE RISE OF THE SAMURAI

From the earliest times, Japan had been ruled by an Emperor. He lived in a rich and splendid palace in Kyoto and was treated almost like a god. But his people never saw him, and his government was very badly organized. By the twelfth century the Emperor started to lose his power and could no longer make the rich and powerful lords obey him. They would not pay their taxes and they refused to give the Emperor soldiers for his army.

The Emperor's government and army became so weak that he could not control crime. The country was filled with bands of robbers. Rich landowners needed protection and they began to recruit their own private armies. The men who served in such armies were called Samurai. The Japanese word *Samurai* means "one who serves." The warriors promised complete loyalty to their lords. These Samurai armies were so powerful that the Emperor began to use them instead of his own soldiers.

The best Samurai sometimes became powerful lords themselves.

Rich landowners hired Samurai warriors to protect them from bands of robbers.

The Samurai leaders grouped together to form rival clans, which often fought wars against each other. The first of these were the Gempei wars between 1180 and 1185, which were won by the Minamoto clan. Their leader, Yoritomo, was given the title *Shogun*, which means "Commander-in-Chief." He was head of all the Samurai warlords. The Shoguns actually ruled Japan for the next seven centuries, although the Emperor was still officially in charge.

THE SAMURAI IN SOCIETY

In the early seventeenth century the highest-placed person in Japan was the Emperor, but the most powerful was the Shogun. The nobles were also important, and the Shogun feared they might challenge his power. He sent spies to watch the nobles. He made them report regularly to his court, and only allowed them to marry women of whom he approved. He also set up checkpoints to search travelers for weapons.

The Shogun depended on the loyalty of the Samurai for his power, so he treated them well and gave them special privileges. Only Samurai were allowed to carry two swords. They were allowed to put ordinary

people to death for the slightest reason whenever they wished. The only people who could become Samurai were the sons of Samurai. This made the Samurai a separate class. They were the most powerful, feared and respected group in Japan.

Next in importance came the farmers and artisans. At first, merchants were not respected by the Samurai, but gradually they became more important, as the Shoguns needed their advice on money and trade.

Ordinary peasants had very little power or freedom. The Shogun Iyeyasu took away many of their rights. They were forbidden to wear any cloth except cotton. They had to give half of their farm produce to the Shogun, so they often went hungry. There were several peasant rebellions, but they were mercilessly crushed by the Samurai.

Left *This seventeenth-century Japanese picture shows Nijo Castle, the home of Shogun Iyeyasu.*

Right *Ordinary peasants in Japan worked hard and had little freedom.*

9

A WARRIOR'S TRAINING

The sons of Samurai were prepared from birth for their future lives as warriors. They attended school and learned reading, writing and good manners, but it was fighting and self-defense that really mattered. At the age of fifteen they were given their first sword in a special ceremony. The young warriors learned the skills of war from their fathers or from the local Samurai master. Sometimes they went away to training schools.

Sword fighting was the most important skill, as the sword was the Samurai's main weapon. Speed and accuracy were needed more than strength. Styles of swordplay copied the movements of animals and birds such as cats, monkeys and swallows. Some sword strokes had special names, such as "torso severer" or "scarf sweep."

A Samurai's training also included unarmed combat skills, particularly wrestling and *ju-jitsu* (similar to modern judo). These could be dangerous, so all students learned how to set broken bones! Some contestants were killed in training.

Archery was important too. The Samurai bow was about 8 feet (2½ meters) long, with razor-sharp arrows that could cut a man's head off. Special halls over 300 feet (100 meters) long were built for archery practice. Sometimes live animals were used as targets. On one occasion 150 dogs were shot down in an arena by 36 mounted bowmen.

Left *A master instructs his pupils in sword fighting. Training to become a Samurai began at an early age.*

Right *Archery was one of the many skills a Samurai learned.*

ARMOR AND WEAPONS

A Samurai's battle-dress was very complicated. A warrior might take up to an hour to get ready. He washed, arranged his hair and perfumed himself. Then he put on a loincloth, *kimono* and baggy trousers (see page 24). Next came the armor. This was made from small overlapping iron plates, tied together with brightly colored cord. A breast plate protected the chest, back and sides, and there were arm gauntlets, leg guards and an iron collar to protect the neck. The armor was suprisingly light – about 25 lb (12 kg) – though it did become heavier in wet weather, when the cords became soaked with water. When firearms were introduced, the iron plates were covered with steel, and more use was made of large pieces of plate armor to give extra protection.

It took so long to strap on all the pieces of armor that the Samurai tried different ways of dressing more quickly. Some hung their suits from the ceiling and lowered them onto their shoulders.

A Samurai's crowning glory was his helmet. It was made of steel, often with horns and a fearsome papier-mâché mask to frighten the enemy. In the sixteenth and seventeenth centuries these masks became more and more terrifying.

A fully-armed Samurai went into battle with a sword, dagger and a spear or bow. When firearms began to be used, fewer Samurai carried bows, as spears were more useful. Firearms were not used by the Samurai themselves, but by foot soldiers.

Left *Japanese artisans making a Samurai's battle-dress and armor.*

A warrior often took as long as an hour to prepare for battle.

13

THE SAMURAI SWORD

A Samurai warrior wore two swords – the *katana*, or long sword, and the *wakizashi*, or short sword. The *katana* was his main battle sword. It was beautifully made by skilled sword-smiths. It was believed that the best swords had supernatural powers, and so swordsmiths had to be men of very good character.

Before beginning to make a blade,

A swordsmith hammered a Samurai sword from a piece of white-hot iron.

the swordsmith prayed to the gods to frighten off any evil spirits. Then he hammered out a lump of white-hot iron, and folded and hammered it again up to twenty times. This produced a blade made of many layers of iron, with a pattern similar to wood grain. The blade was then worked so that the cutting edge was

The hilt of a Samurai sword was richly decorated. This example, made in copper gilt, is inlaid with hundreds of tiny pearls.

This seventeenth-century picture shows a Samurai testing his sword in battle. It had to be very sharp!

harder than the rest of the blade. This edge was sharpened and tested on iron sheets, armor and sometimes dead criminals before the sword was sold. A Samurai expected his sword to cut off an enemy's head with just one stroke!

The blade was often decorated with designs such as dragons. The hilt would be covered with gold and jewels, and the sheath was made from lacquered wood, ivory or leather. Swords were given names like "beard-biter" and "knee-severer."

A sword might pass from father to son, together with stories of its deeds in battle.

INTO BATTLE

The Samurai rode into battle on strong but small Japanese horses, not huge war horses. Their harnesses and saddles were beautifully decorated, and their colorful saddle-cloths often had tassles reaching to the ground.

In the traditional way of fighting, the battle began with individual duels between opposing Samurai. Champions challenged each other to single combat, calling out their names, family history and deeds in battle. After the duels, all the Samurai and foot soldiers went into battle. The more heads a Samurai could cut off, the greater his honor. Sometimes, the opening duels did not take place, and the battle began immediately. Battles were hard to organize in bad weather or at night.

In 1543, the Portugese came to Japan and brought with them a kind of gun called an *arquebus*. This amazed the Japanese, but it was soon being used by foot soldiers in place of the bow. Because of this new weapon, methods of fighting gradually changed. In 1575, there was a famous battle at Nagashino.

Before the main battle began, individual duels were often fought.

General Nobunaga held his Samurai back until the enemy horsemen were very near. He then gave the order for his foot soldiers to fire, and won the battle easily. From that time, all Japanese generals used similar tactics.

Samurai women sometimes went into battle, fighting alongside their husbands and fellow warriors. They learned to perfect a type of combat called *naginata*. This used a weapon made from a piece of hardwood about 6 feet (1.8 meters) long, to which was attached a very sharp blade. From 1600 onward, this type of fighting was left totally to women, and some Samurai enemies were reported to have lost a limb in such a conflict!

JAPANESE CASTLES

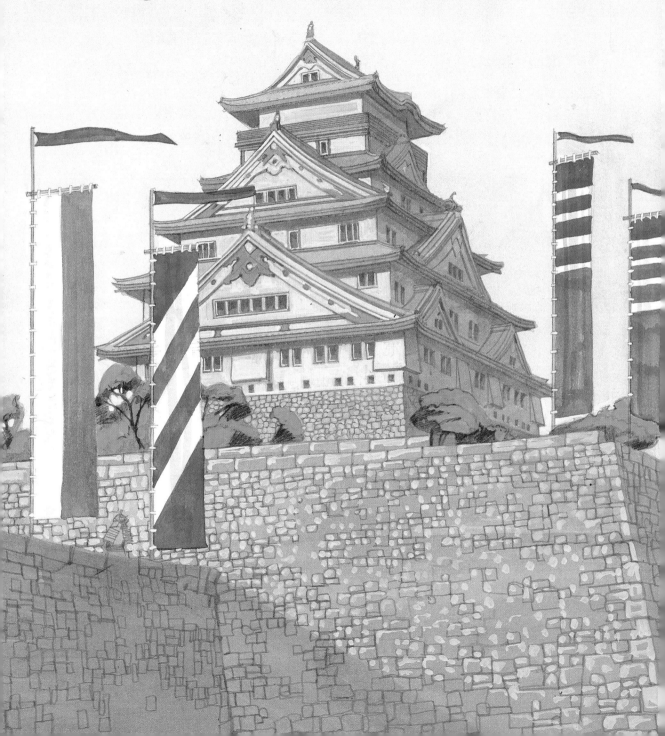

Japanese castles were much more beautiful and comfortable than those found in Europe at the time. They were usually built on a hill. The foundations were made of rock, and the upper part of wood. At the top was the keep, which might be many stories high. The lord and his family lived in great comfort in the inner keep.

The walls and towers of the castle were elegantly decorated, and the tiled roof of the keep often had gold-painted ornaments. The castle grounds were planted with trees and shrubs, and there were artifical lakes covered with beautiful plants such as lilies. In spite of their beauty, the castles were very well protected. There were deep moats around the grounds. The gates were overlooked by holes through which boiling liquids could be poured on any attackers. All the windows were barred, and there were slits in the walls for firing arrows and guns.

The best way to break into a castle was by a surprise attack. If this failed, there might be a long siege,

Left *Japanese castles were built to withstand attack. A large moat surrounded the castle grounds.*

Sieges were common in seventeenth-century Japan. This painting depicts a scene from the siege of Osaka Castle in 1615.

waiting for the people inside to run out of food or water. Ladders were used to scale the walls, and often armies tried to tunnel underneath.

There was a special group of Samurai called the *Ninja*, who were trained as spies and assassins. They dressed in black and entered castles secretly at night, to carry out murder.

RELIGION AND THE SAMURAI CODE

One of the oldest Japanese religions is Shinto. Its followers believed in the spirits of the nature-gods – gods of the trees, flowers, rocks, rivers and mountains. The most important of these was Amateratsu, the sun goddess. Every Japanese village had a shrine to a particular god or goddess.

In the sixth century, Chinese monks introduced the teachings of Buddha and Confucius. Many Samurai became Buddhists. Most belonged to the Zen-Buddhist group.

They believed that men could control events in their lives through meditation. They spent many hours in meditation to develop inner strength and knowledge. Some Samurai did not like the strict life of a Zen-Buddhist. Instead, they believed in Lord Amida, the Buddha

If a Samurai lost his honor through surrender or cowardice, he would usually commit hara-kiri, *a ritual suicide.*

of Boundless Life. He was an Indian Prince, who was supposed to lead his followers to a paradise above the clouds. This religion had no rules, only the belief in Lord Amida.

In 1543 European missionaries brought Christianity to Japan, and many Samurai became Christians. At times, Christians were cruelly treated by those who followed other religions.

The warrior code, or *bushido*, was more important to a Samurai than any religion. The main aims of a warrior were honor in battle and loyalty to his lord. Cowardice or surrender meant loss of honor. A Samurai who had lost his honor was expected to kill himself in the ritual of *seppuku* or *hara-kiri*. He used his short sword to cut open his abdomen. It was believed that this released his spirit.

Above right *Lord Amida, the Buddha of Boundless Life. Some Samurai preferred to believe in this less-strict form of Buddhism.*

Right *Temples, like this one in Kyoto, were an ideal place for the Samurai to meditate and develop inner strength.*

AT HOME

The houses of Samurai were wooden buildings with sloping roofs supported on large pillars. The roofs were covered with shingles, tiles or thatch. The outside walls were made from bamboo sticks covered with plaster or daub (a mixture of clay and cow dung!).

The floors were raised off the ground to keep the house dry in wet weather. They were covered with rectangular straw mats called *tatami*. The kitchen was the only room with an earth floor. The shape of the rooms inside could be changed by moving the interior wall panels along grooves in the floor. Beautiful printed screens were also used to make a room more private. The master of the house slept on a thick mattress, surrounded by curtains. There

was little furniture, only a few low tables, straw cushions and bamboo chests.

The bathroom was separate from the rest of the house. The Samurai liked to relax in hot baths, but they always washed first. The tea house might also be built away from the main part of the house. Here the ritual of the tea ceremony was performed (see page 28).

The Samurai enjoyed gardening, and made beautiful water gardens with ornamental lakes and streams. They also made mysterious rock and sand gardens where they would sit and meditate. Samurai homes had to be protected against attack. The courtyard was surrounded by a high wall, and there was usually a watch-tower near the main gate. Warriors often lived in the outbuildings.

A warrior's home. Warriors enjoyed creating rock gardens, as seen in the foreground of this picture.

FASHION AND CLOTHING

Personal appearance was very important to a Samurai. When relaxing at home he wore kimono – a long-sleeved garment like a dressing gown, belted around the waist. He always kept two swords in his belt when he was outdoors. Under the kimono he wore another similar garment and loose-fitting trousers. On formal occasions he wore a padded jacket, often decorated with his family crest.

The wives of the Samurai wore up to five kimonos, one on top of another, tied with a sash. Each one opened at the front to show the color of the kimono underneath. Women usually wore red trousers. Both men and women wore straw sandals in fine weather and wooden clogs in wet weather.

Samurai warriors had long hair, which was combed back, tied in a pony tail and doubled over. Many shaved the front half of their heads, and small beards or moustaches were common. Women always had very

Examples of different Samurai family crests.

long hair, which often reached to their feet. They sometimes used false hair pieces. They plucked or shaved their eyebrows and painted false ones higher up. Pale faces were considered beautiful, so ladies always kept out of the sun. They whitened their faces with ground rice and white lead. The lead must have poisoned many of them. Both men and women blackened their teeth. They thought that white teeth looked naked and ugly.

A Samurai family dressed in formal clothes at home. The Samurai's jacket was often embroidered with his family crest.

FOOD AND DRINK

In wartime the Samurai ate two meals a day, which were mainly rice dishes. They also ate dried fish and vegetables, seaweed and pickled plums. The rice was stuffed into bamboo tubes or rolled in leaves and

Foot soldiers preparing food in wartime.

then roasted. When there was no fire for cooking, the rice was wrapped in a cloth, soaked in water and eaten raw. Rice was the basic food in peacetime too, but a greater variety of meat, fish, seaweed and vegetables was available. Most food was cooked in vegetable oil and was richly flavored.

There were strict rules about cooking methods, the utensils used and how the food was eaten. Mealtimes could be rather awkward as it was thought rude to start eating first or to finish last. The men ate sitting on the floor, separated from the women. Their food was served on small trays by servants or wives, who had to hold the trays above their heads, so they did not breathe on the food.

The Japanese believed that certain foods had special powers. To bring luck before going into battle, a Samurai warrior ate *awabi* (shellfish) and *kombu* (seaweed with chestnuts), and drank *sake*. Sake was their main drink, made from fermented rice. It was very alcoholic. Green leaf tea was also drunk with a meal or after it. A special powdered tea was used for the tea ceremony.

At home the Samurai enjoyed a wide variety of food.

GAMES AND PASTIMES

Many of the sporting pastimes of the Samurai helped prepare them for war. These includes hunting, swimming and wrestling. A game similar to soccer was also very popular, played on a square field with very complicated rules. Another game was *Go*, which was played on a board with black and white stones, rather like chess.

Although the Samurai were very brutal in war, they enjoyed such things as poetry writing and flower arranging when at home. Incense-burning competitions were held, to see who could recognize the greatest number of different incense smells.

The tea ceremony was very important to the Samurai. It was held in a special tea house set aside for the purpose. There were strict rules for making the tea, preparing the food

Warriors enjoyed visiting the Noh *theater, where actors danced and mimed while a story was sung.*

and reading certain poems during the ceremony. All Samurai aimed to perfect this ceremony, which was often held straight after a fierce battle.

Because of their special place in society, the Samurai were discouraged from going to the theater. However, many did visit the *Noh* theater. The actors wore richly decorated costumes and masks, which told the audience what sort of character they were playing. The actors danced and

A seventeenth-century tea house in Japan. Here warriors learned to perfect the ritual of the tea ceremony.

mimed without scenery, while the story was sung. The plays were often about the brave deeds of warriors.

One pastime that the Shoguns tried to stop was gambling. A Samurai could lose his weapons, armor and horses on the throw of the dice.

THE SAMURAI TRADITION

The power of the Samurai was over well before 1900, but Samurai beliefs have affected Japanese life long after this time. During World War II, for example, Japanese soldiers would fight to the death rather than surrender. Their cruelty toward prisoners of war was misguidedly explained by the Samurai belief that a captured soldier had lost his honor.

Even in the present day, Japanese workers show the same loyalty and devotion to their employers as the Samurai showed to his lord, and many Japanese who have suffered failure or disgrace choose to commit suicide rather than live without honor. The Samurai no longer rule Japan, but their beliefs and ideas are far from dead.

1900: The end of an era. Samurai warriors in European clothes, their power as the most feared and repected class in Japan had finally faded.

30

GLOSSARY

Arquebus An early firearm, loaded through the muzzle and supported on a forked rest when fired.

Artisans People, such as carpenters and blacksmiths, who make things by hand.

Gauntlet An arm guard, for the lower arm, made from small iron plates.

Hilt The handle of a sword or dagger.

Incense A gum or spice that produces a sweet smell when burned.

Merchant A trader who buys and sells goods.

Meditation A kind of mental exercise in which people sit in silence for long periods, concentrating on a particular idea or object.

Papier mâché A hard, strong material made from layers of paper mixed with paste.

Privileges Special treatment or benefits.

Recruit To enlist, or hire, a soldier.

Ritual A set way of performing a religious act.

White lead A white powder made from lead and used as make-up.

MORE BOOKS TO READ

A Family in Japan, Judith Elkin (Lerner, 1987)

Japan, Karen Jacobsen (Children's Press, 1982)

Take a Trip to Japan, Gwynneth Ashby (Franklin Watts, 1981)

We Live in Japan, Kazuhide Kawamata (Franklin Watts, 1984)

Picture acknowledgments

The pictures in this book were supplied by the following: Peter Newark's Western Americana 30; Ronald Sheridan's Photo Library 11, 21, (top); Victoria and Albert Museum 15 (bottom), 27; Werner Forman Archive 5, 8, 12, 15 (top), 19, 21 (bottom), 29. The artwork on page 24 is by Malcolm S. Walker.

INDEX

© Copyright 1986 Wayland (Publishers) Limited
61 Western Road, Hove, East Sussex,
BN3 1JD, England